Essentials for Cultivating Passionate Volunteers and Leaders

Guidelines for Organizations that Value Connection

Eddie Zacapa

LIFE ENRICHING
BOOKS

San Jose, CA

Life Enriching Books, Permissions Dept.
2056 Villagetree Dr., San Jose, CA 95131
Tel: 916-409-0879

Essentials for Cultivating Passionate Volunteers and Leaders: Guidelines for Organizations that Value Connection — 1st edition

ISBN: 978-0-9994170-0-3 (Paperback edition)
ISBN: 978-0-9994170-1-0 (eBook edition)

Author: Eddie Zacapa
Editor: Laura Hauge

Printed in the United States of America

1st Printing, October 2018

Praise for *Essentials for Cultivating Passionate Volunteers and Leaders*

"Eddie offers practical ideas, inspirational stories and powerful support for finding and retaining volunteers to enrich and enhance your organization's goals. His ideas and delightful examples spring from his experience and varied learning over many years of cultivating and nurturing volunteers and leaders."
Sylvia Haskvitz, CNVC trainer and assessor, author of Eat by Choice, Not by Habit and contributing author of Healing Our Planet, Healing Ourselves

"This book relates to "best practices" for leadership; relationships with employees, building a business/organizational culture where people look forward to coming to work and focus on not just doing their best but extending their responsibilities to making all stakeholders valuable human beings - each with a purpose or gift to bring to the table! I love the book, it is at the same time inspiring and practical!"
Susie Davies, Chief Executive Officer, Mother Lode Rehabilitation Enterprises

"Eddie Zacapa's book applies key principles of Nonviolent Communication to cultivating and maintaining volunteers for your organization, including connecting with intrinsic purpose, giving effective feedback, and the role of appreciation (gratitude). It also is full of practical advice. A useful guide for anyone working with volunteers and desiring to do so with greater effectiveness, connection, and compassion."

Dian Killian, CNVC Certified Trainer and author,
Connecting across Differences: How to Connect with
Anyone, Anytime, Anywhere

"This guide will help any organization that is looking for long term volunteers to bulk up their staff with heart."

Gloria Webster, Volunteer

"Reading Eddie's book brought up so many emotions. I have known Eddie for a few years and I can attest to his commitment, passion, professionalism and compassion. In this book, he shares his own experiences on how to lay down a fertile space for volunteers and dissects the importance to nurture them in a kind and respectful manner. Eddie provides concise examples on how to provide a bounty of opportunities not only for volunteers but for the community they serve. The book is insightful and inspiring."

Ruth Zermeño-Rodriguez,
Peer Counselor, Family Advocate

"Eddie powerfully lifts up the concepts of 'love thy neighbor' in this book. He illustrates how volunteering time and skills to our communities teaches teamwork, communication, conflict resolution, critical thinking, project planning and other important life skills. Eddie especially captures how human beings can bring out the best in each other through volunteerism. He also reminds us to preserve and treasure our interconnectedness as global citizens."

Ami Pascual Spear
Founding Executive Director, South of Market Foundation
Community Economic Development practitioner

"No one who works with volunteers should miss reading *Essentials for Cultivating Passionate Volunteers and Leaders*. Eddie speaks from rich experience and a compassionate heart. The "essentials" he provides are spectacular for both their simplicity and depth! The book is remarkable for its brevity and comprehensiveness. It will become a core manual for leading volunteers in our church. In my humble opinion, Eddie is like our Santa Claus (*you'll have to read the book for this to make complete sense*) because he is giving our leaders the opportunity to serve, grow and contribute to our volunteers."

Karl Ortis, Pastor,
Western Hills Church

"Eddie does a wonderful job touching on important aspects of inspiring volunteers and retaining them. Each idea is supported with real-life experiences, which help the readers understand the concept in depth. From building leadership skills to forming relationships and a sense of belonging, Eddie shares his expertise and knowledge for all agencies and organizations who work with volunteers. A must read for everyone involved in community engagement services!"

Yoko Kono, Outreach Coordinator,
Hands 4 Hope

Dedication

To my mother, Lavinia Zacapa,
who has always been there for me.

To Mercy Housing for giving me the opportunity
to cultivate volunteers.

To all the volunteers I have worked with and who have
made a difference in other's lives, including mine.

To Marshall Rosenberg for bringing Nonviolent Communication to the world. His communication process
and approach to life have had an enormous impact on
my life and on this book.

To my wife Gaby, who is my best friend and offers me
support in so many ways.

To my boys, Adam and Andrew, for inspiring me –
I want to create a better world for you.

TABLE OF CONTENTS

PREFACE

This book is meant to be a guide to help and support anyone who works with volunteers and/or wants to develop a volunteer program. It is also a good read for anyone who volunteers or has an interest in volunteering. For instance, a volunteer can read this book and get an idea about what to look for in an organization that has a volunteer program. Also, it is suggested that organizations that are practicing the principles mentioned in the book share these with their volunteers so that everyone gets the most out of their experience.

Finding and cultivating quality volunteers is not easy. Many organizations are looking for volunteers to help them provide services and fulfill their mission. Yet, there seems to be a scarcity when it comes to finding volunteers, and when found, retaining them is another challenge.

This book will help you find volunteers, train them, and increase your chances of keeping them long term. I will draw from my 20 years of experience working with volunteers in nonprofits and assist you in building a team of volunteers. I currently work as a Resident Services Coordinator with Mercy Housing and will, at times, give examples from my experiences with volunteers and our team. I will also give examples of other work experiences I have had along the way.

The book was designed to cut to the chase (so to speak) and highlight key points that can help the reader find, cultivate and support volunteers. My desire was to keep this book short so that the reader could reference key points when needed after the first read. The book can be applied to any business, non-profit organization, group or individual that endeavors to work with volunteers.

So, let's get started.

CHAPTER ONE

BUILDING COMMUNITY

"Within the community, friendship is the habit that binds people together when they take pleasure in each other's company, listen, laugh, and share good times or bad."
—Clifton Taulbert

I recall the first time I volunteered in college. I volunteered at my local church and led the young adult group. I was so excited to join a cause and be a part of something that I believed in. It meant a lot to me to be around other people who also really cared about making a difference. I made friends and connections that I would never forget. I am still in touch with some of the people I volunteered with, worked with and served. The thing that I enjoyed the most was the sense of being a part of something bigger than myself and being a part of a community.

When a person decides to volunteer with an organization they are joining a common cause. They are becoming partners with the organization to do something together with others and will be in frequent company with staff, and possibly with other volunteers, to accomplish certain common goals. There will be shared values, goals and expectations. Every volunteer or staff member who joins the team is part of the community and culture of the organization. A community consists of a group of individuals who share common interests and goals and who do life together. There is a level of caring for each other that is lived out. When people are a part of community they feel connected and experience a sense of mattering.

Community is the glue to building an effective and united team of volunteers and staff. Community involves caring about each other's needs and being there for each other. It is about mourning together and celebrating together. It involves spending time with each other and having fun together.

I recall a time where one of the volunteers on our team lost a very special friend. Many of the members of our team assisted and attended a funeral on our site to honor her friend. We were there for her when she needed support.

As a program coordinator, I have always tried to come up with a team name for volunteers and staff who will be working together. For instance, in one of my jobs we formed the Positive Solutions Team. Our motto was to create positive solutions together to help others. We met monthly and included both volunteers and staff at these meetings. Everyone had an equal voice. Many of our best ideas and feedback came from volunteers. Whenever possible, try to invite volunteers to participate in team meetings where they can voice their ideas and concerns. It provides an opportunity for participation that gives a sense of belonging, and that creates a sense of ownership. They are officially a part of the team, not outsiders.

At White Rock Village, a property of Mercy Housing, all individuals who volunteered were a part of the Community Care Team (CCT). The CCT team was formed in collaboration with volunteers and staff. Volunteers were a part of its formation and their ideas came to life as it unfolded.

Each volunteer who joined the team received a T-Shirt that read, "Community Care Team" on the front and "Doing our Neighbor Good" on the back. The T-Shirts recognized the volunteers as a resource in the community. When we had events, volunteers wore the shirts and were easily identified as individuals who could be approached for help. The volunteers wore the T-shirts with pride.

We had scheduled trainings and/or retreats for volunteers and staff. Many times trainings bring unity of purpose and bring the team closer. You can schedule something off-site or on-site. You can determine whatever works best for your situation. If you offer a training, you can have staff provide the training and/or have a guest speaker come and do a presentation.

Cultivating Potential Relationships

A volunteer offers support and help in doing tasks that help you and your organization fulfill your mission. Volunteers are looking to work with organizations or groups that are doing something meaningful and that allow them to make a difference. When individuals decide to volunteer, they will co-labor with the organization to fulfill a service that the organization is passionate about. Conveying the mission and purpose of the organization early on is essential to establishing a good working relationship with volunteers and furthering the message. Volunteers may be working with you directly or on your team and may be representing your organization in the community.

When you ask someone to volunteer, you are adding a new member to your team and you are offering them an opportunity to be a part of your cause. In a work environment that means they will experience the work culture, interact with staff and clients and become a part of that dynamic.

Having someone volunteer with your organization is not just about getting someone to do work, it is about engaging an individual to fulfill a purpose and need and supporting them in their goals. In this process, needs will be fulfilled.

Marshall Rosenberg, the founder and director of educational services for the Center for Nonviolent Communication, an international peacemaking organization, believed that everything human beings do is in service of meeting needs. He believed that needs are universal and he made a distinction between needs and strategies. This distinction between needs and strategies is important to make because strategies are what we do or ask others to do to meet our needs. Strategies can include asking someone to do something that will satisfy one of our needs. If we believe that a strategy is a need we may also get attached to that strategy and not be able to see other options for meeting our needs.

It is important to remember a volunteer can help fulfill a need for an organization, but that a volunteer or volunteers are not a need. They provide a way to meet a need. For instance, your needs for help, support, ease, balance, and outreach may be met. For the volunteer, their needs for contribution, meaning, connection and belonging may be fulfilled.

Recruiting volunteers is a strategy for meeting needs that an organization may have identified. Needs are values that we all have. We all need support, connection, meaning, ease, balance, respect, understanding and advocacy. How we go about meeting these needs specifically involves strategies. For example, posting a job description on Volunteer Match would be a strategy for meeting the need for support, advocacy, and teamwork that a group of individuals who are a part of an organization have. Another example would be someone taking out the trash. The act of taking out the trash is a strategy for meeting the need for cleanliness.

Every volunteer also has needs they are trying to fulfill. To become aware of what those are and advocate for those needs goes a long way when it comes to them feeling comfortable and supported within the organization.

Mr. Gordon Bethune, retired U.S. airline executive and former CEO of Continental Airlines, said, "I like to think that a lot of managers and executives trying to solve problems miss the forest for the trees by forgetting to look at their people – not at how much more they can get from their people or how they can more effectively manage their people. I think they need to look a little more closely at what it's like for their people to work there every day."[1]

This goes for volunteers, as well. Sometimes managers can be caught up on the single-minded type of thinking that focuses on attaining effective outcomes or results and an attachment to one strategy to attain those results. Sometimes what can occur is that we can become "blinded by the prize." When we open our hearts to what our employees and volunteers are experiencing and listening to their feedback, we demonstrate that we care, and we cultivate a culture of caring. I will focus more on this on the chapter titled *Developing a Culture of Empathy*.

Of course, every organization longs to find people who are productive, hard-working and have the ability and skills to continually develop their potential. Yet, it is important to also nurture a climate where everyone's needs matter and are held collectively. A climate where all the parties involved have a voice and where feedback is received from all sides. The downside of not nurturing this culture is long-term losses that involve losing star-employees or volunteers and high turnover. Loss of staff can lead to further costs and later failures.

When you add someone to your team, they will be in relationship with you and others. You will want to tend to that relationship and check-in on them to make sure they are adapting well to the team, the work culture and/or department. I recommend contacting them within a few days from their start date and continually having someone check in weekly or bi-weekly once they are trained.

I remember calling one of our volunteers on the phone who was helping with after school programming and he really appreciated me calling to just check in. He shared with me some concerns he had, I made some suggestions, and he had a sense of really being supported. He thanked me for calling him and offering him my support. Many times, a phone call can let a volunteer know that you care about them and their progress and that they are not alone.

By listening to volunteers, being proactive in making sure they are adapting to the work environment and providing them leadership and support in learning the ropes, you are developing trust, connection and mutual respect.

CHAPTER TWO

NATURAL GIVING

All of us enjoy giving to others. It is a need we all have. Sometimes I have found that volunteers may be more connected to this desire to give than employees. They are excited and filled with anticipation, while employees sometimes get bogged down with the work and see their tasks and responsibilities as mundane. Of course, we hope that is not the case, and sometimes the volunteer with his or her enthusiasm can bring a positive spark to other employees with their enthusiasm and excitement. It is important to engage volunteers during this honeymoon period before they lose their enthusiasm. I have seen volunteers lost because staff did not engage and direct volunteers to opportunities quick enough. I recommend plugging volunteers into the appropriate serving opportunities as soon as possible. If you wait a few weeks to reach out to them, they may lose the excitement and desire to volunteer with your agency and go elsewhere.

Volunteers are looking for the opportunity to enrich life and contribute in some capacity. They are very connected to that longing as they anticipate joining an agency.

I once heard the story told of a child living in poverty in Great Britain during World War I. The little boy was waiting by a donut shop one morning, looking through the glass at the donuts. His eyes were wide open and as big as apples as he stared at the donuts. A soldier walked into the donut shop and   bought a dozen donuts. As he walked out he noticed the boy, handed the dozen donuts to him and started to walk away. The boy stands stunned for a moment and then runs after the soldier and pulls on his coat. The soldier turns around and looks down at the little boy. The boy looks up at the soldier and asks the soldier, "Are you God?"

It turns out that someone told the boy that if he prayed to God, his prayers would be answered. It turns out the boy prayed to be able to have a donut that morning. The soldier answered his prayer. Who doesn't want to be an answer to prayer?

It is a wonderful feeling to be able to help others and contribute in some way. Volunteers are in touch with this feeling and they are looking for opportunities to bless others. We do well to be aware of this and to light their fire.

Whenever possible, we can ask volunteers what they are passionate about and use that information to find the best role for them. For instance, if you want someone to tutor kids but the volunteer you are interviewing wants to teach music, it makes more sense to create an opportunity for them to do that or to be honest with them about what the options are for them. It is not about getting people to do a task, it is about honoring who they are and holding that with them to find them a role that really fits for them. They will be happier if this is considered and when they are working out of their giftedness and passion, those they serve will benefit, as well.

To work with others to fulfill a mission or goal is a sacred process. Making something sacred means preparing and creating a safe vessel, a container for others to join in. This space is a place where we trust and hold with others what is precious to us. It is the formation of community. When we achieve this, we can bless others and heal the world. Asking volunteers to join us and become a part of what we are doing is a special event and an opportunity for collaboration to happen. To not realize unity could very well mean missing an opportunity for the cultivation of community and collaboration to work at its best. Finding common purpose with others is exciting to be a part of; it's special and important. It is not something we rush into.

Asking vs. Guilt Tripping

Sometimes asking others for help does not come easy to us. We may be worried that we may come across as if we are trying to twist someone's arm to help us. We may also think that we are bothering the person by asking them to help or that they might just say "yes" because they feel obligated. These thoughts, if we give in to them, will lead us to not ask others for help.

Yet, when we are asking people to volunteer, it is like we are Santa Claus because we are giving people various opportunities to serve, grow and contribute. We have an opportunity to help others find their purpose. What can be better than that?

Trying to make others feel guilty or obligate them is not necessary. It is true that some people have used guilt tripping to ask others for help. But it rarely works and even if it does, it usually leads to resentment and disappointment. When we realize that most people want to contribute to a cause, it becomes easier to just simply ask.

As we engage with potential volunteers and future volunteers, it is helpful to keep in mind to use language that gives choice. No one likes being told what to do. Try to use phrases like, "Would you be willing to…" or "I am wondering if you could…" or "Would you consider…" instead of phrases like, "I need you to…" or "We really need help and I think you should volunteer" or "Go over there and be helpful." The latter are uses of demand language. It is good to use language that gives people choices and this goes for employees, as well.

When we realize that others want to team up with us, it can bring a spring back in our step. It is exciting for the volunteer because they now have an opportunity to use their talents to help others. It is exciting for us because with more volunteers we can accomplish more, fulfill the mission of our organization, help more people, and build meaningful connections. It is also exciting for us (the one who asks) because we get to give others an opportunity to make a difference. We all have a desire to contribute to life. It is a vital need that we all want to fulfill and when we have a chance to live that out we feel more complete.

I can't tell you how many times I have seen people light up right in front of my eyes when I ask them to volunteer in some capacity. It is like they just found their way home. I think that it is because someone noticed them and they believed in themselves to make a difference. A positive experience of connection may meet a longing for mattering, significance and to be a part of something bigger than themselves. It is vital for volunteers to feel connected to a team or community and the more they experience this bond, the longer they will stay committed to the cause.

So, as you go looking for volunteers, do a heart check and remember that you have an opportunity to be a blessing to others by asking them to help you or your cause. If you are feeling bogged down and like the job is getting mundane, ask yourself how what you are doing is contributing to making life better for others.

The Need for Play

Rosenberg, who was the 2006 recipient of the Global Village Foundation's Bridge of Peace Award and has traveled all over the world helping others resolve conflicts, said, "Don't do anything that isn't play."

What I think he meant was to always be connected to why you are doing something and what need of yours is being fulfilled as you do it. I think that when we do this, we cannot help but experience joy, and as a result, whatever the activity is, it becomes fun.

I also encourage you to think of ways that you can bring more fun to the work environment. Ice breakers between staff and volunteers are vital to building teamwork and providing the space for fun and play. Incorporating games during trainings can lead to relieving office pressures and the expression of natural talents. Collaboration has a recharging effect. Some work environments have a ping pong table or game room. Going for walks together can also be a way to connect and incorporate movement and exercise.

A poem I wrote captures, for me, the beauty of play and the experience of joy connected to it.

Make Time to Play
By Eddie Zacapa
7/16/12

When we play we feel glee, lighthearted and free.
It is a time of fun, laughter and suspense.
Our cares grow wings and fly away.
Grace abounds.
Life is good.

Fun is here to stay.
Time stops when we play.
All that matters is enjoying each other's company.
Balloons, face painting, costumes, fake tattoos and games are
what we do.

Play reminds us to enjoy life, to forget the negative.
We are at one with life - lost in bliss.

Don't forget to play, learn from the little ones.
Make time to play - to draw, to paint, to chase or dance.
You might get lost in a trance.
You just might find the child in you.
You might just get a second chance.

When we are playful and having fun, we are being motivated from within. We are not being coerced or pressured to
do anything. We are free and in harmony with our needs. The
more we can live in that place - no matter wherever we find
ourselves - the more joy we will experience in our lives. And
when we are experiencing that joy in a work environment,
contribution and service just flows like a river.

If we find ourselves stuck in "I have to" thinking, we can re-
place that with the phrase, "I choose to because…" You can fin-
ish the latter phrase with a quality or need that will be fulfilled.
For instance, you may say, "I choose to enter this data because
it contributes to being able to track efforts and outcomes and
helps bring to light the work I do." You may want to say it
a couple times so that it sinks in. This is something I learned
from Marshall Rosenberg and have experienced a major shift
when I do it.

Remembering why you are doing something versus telling yourself you "have to" do something will change your whole outlook on a task. This will also help you share "why" with volunteers.

CHAPTER THREE

APPROACHES FOR CHOOSING VOLUNTEERS

There are different approaches and strategies to inviting volunteers to join your organization or cause. One approach is like casting a net. For instance, if you have an event that you are doing with your organization, you can have a scheduled time during the event to share the need you have that volunteers can assist with. This allows you to hold that need together with others and to potentially reach more people. You can ask individuals to contact you at a specific time if they would like to volunteer. It could be that they come up to a table and talk to you during or after the event. You can also have a volunteer form ready with different needs and have people mark down what they might be interested in doing. They can turn those forms in to you or in a box. Sometimes this will bring in volunteers and other times it will not. This approach is all about casting a large net to see if anyone happens to want to volunteer with your organization or cause. Another way to do this can be to put an ad on CraigsList or Volunteer Match or other websites that can further your reach. This makes the opportunity available to even more people.

When you do meet with someone who has answered an ad, it is still helpful to explore with them what their passion is and to build a relationship. Yet, relying only on ads can limit the potential to attain more volunteers and to be able to have a greater reach in helping others through your work or cause.

Another approach consists of taking advantage of every opportunity to get to talk to people about your need. You never know who might be your next volunteer. Sometimes by just hearing about your need, volunteers spring up from the ground. They may ask you if you are looking for a volunteer or if they can help. Don't be passive. Once you share the need, feel free to ask them if they think they might be interested.

You can ask, "Would you like to help with that?" or "Is that something that you would like to do?" There are many ways to ask and it is good to be clear about the need and how it will make an impact. When you are talking to someone, be thinking, "Is this someone who could be a volunteer?" You won't believe how many times someone you would not have thought to be interested, is actually very excited to know how they can help.

You can tell them about your organization, your goals and the needs you have that volunteers can help fulfill. This will give them more information to consider and help them determine if the task is a good fit for them. You can ask them if they think they can help with your program or need and ask them if they would be interested in considering becoming a volunteer. You can say, "We have been remodeling our Youth Room and provide homework club on Tuesdays and Thursdays at 3:30 pm. We are short staffed and could really use more support. Do you think you might be up to volunteering as a tutor on either of those days?"

The person may say "No," but at least you know that you did not miss an opportunity. You would be surprised how many times people say "Yes."

Key thought to remember: Ask, ask, ask for help. See every interaction as a chance to ask for help from a potential volunteer and to bless them with an opportunity to serve.

Partnerships

Another way to get volunteers to your organization is to develop partnerships with other nonprofits. You can reach out to local churches, the Girl Scouts, colleges in the area, etc. In our county there is an organization called Hands 4 Hope that consists of encouraging youth to volunteer for nonprofits. Mercy Housing partnered with this organization and it generated a lot of youth who volunteered in our after-school programs.

I also established a partnership with a local church in the area that organized a block party for our residents and during Christmas time donated a $25 gift card to every household in the apartment complex. This church also had 22 volunteers come on Serve Day and performed a clean-up project on the property.

You can also partner with schools. There are local high schools that many times have teens who want to volunteer to tutor kids. At a Mercy Housing property, we had some volunteers come and offer their time with the children - a result of reaching out to a local school. Rescue Union School District, another organization we partnered with, provided a summer lunch program on one of our properties and fed our kids lunch for the summer.

As you can see, networking and reaching out to local nonprofits and organizations can really make a difference in making things happen in your community. Uniting with other groups can further your cause within your organization.

CHAPTER FOUR

CONNECTING INDIVIDUALS TO PROJECTS

A ny time you meet someone, you can share your need and ask them if they might be willing to help. When you do this you are offering individuals chances to contribute to your program, enrich their lives and enrich the lives of others. People want to help and make a difference and many times it is simply about finding the right role for them to thrive.

On one occasion, I met a new resident at the affordable housing complex where I work and struck up a conversation with him about sports. It turned out he was a big Sacramento Kings fan. I told him we occasionally got free tickets to games for residents and he was very excited and told me to put him on the list. I did so and a few days later was able to provide him with tickets. He came back after the game and told me all about the game. I then proceeded to show him our youth room and the ping pong table and foosball table in the room. He was immediately drawn to the ping pong table. I told him that we had a need for volunteers for our KidZone program and asked him if he would like to help. He said he would think about it. The next day he said he wanted to volunteer. He was very excited to be able to give back. He wore his volunteer t-shirt proudly and was very committed to volunteering for our program. This example also stresses the importance of building relationships. If we are willing to listen to others and extend our ear and our time, people feel connected to us and feel that they matter. In turn, they become interested in hearing about what matters to us.

Another keen approach to connecting is to be perceptive about what a person's passion is. Everyone has something they are passionate about or skilled in. You can ask questions like, "What do you like to do? What are you passionate about?" By exploring questions like this, people have an opportunity to share with you what they really enjoy. Who doesn't like talking about what they are interested in and excited about? If there is something that is in alignment with a particular service you provide, you can ask them if they would be willing to consider helping you in that specific area.

In my role at Mercy Housing I met a group of knitters who wanted to meet in our community room to knit caps. One of them was willing to teach a class and wanted to donate caps to newborns and to cancer patients. I encouraged them to start a knitting team, and together we came up with a name for the team and a plan for donating caps to local hospitals and organizations. In this situation, the volunteers came to me, but still needed someone to guide them and to provide the space and resources needed to fulfill their goals. They donated over 1,000 caps to newborns and cancer patients within a year of starting their team and their story was featured in the local newspaper and a television show called, "Good Morning Sacramento."

One of the ladies who knit said, "The reason I help is really a selfish reason. It feels good to volunteer and help others. I like to share something that makes me feel good with others so that they can experience it as well."

Many times people are passionate about something and experience the positive effects of participating in a function they simply find delight in, sharing their joy with other individuals.

For example, I met a kid who loved playing soccer. Every time I saw him he had a soccer ball. We got to talking and I encouraged him to start a soccer clinic. He said he wanted me to do it with him. I said okay and we offered a soccer clinic every year in the summer. Many of the kids who participated in the clinic learned basic soccer skills and went on to play in youth soccer leagues.

The youth leader said, "It is meaningful for me to give back because I was once the kid getting the help. This property has helped me with my homework, provided positive role models and assisted us with our housing. I am grateful and want to give back."

Another volunteer who led the art program said, "What I like most about working with the kids is sharing my passion and love for art."

These individuals had one thing in common - they shared the passion they had in their heart with others. When this happens, it is magical to watch. Hold with tenderness the sacred process of finding roles for volunteers that align them with their gifts and talents.

CHAPTER FIVE

GETTING OUT OF COMFORT ZONES

To provide more services and reach more people we need more members to join the team. Yet, we may struggle with asking others to volunteer because we may be shy or afraid of experiencing rejection. If this is the case, we may need to identify the underlying need, which may possibly be for acceptance, confidence, meaningful connections and/or mattering. If we can realize that our acceptance or needs do not rely on others saying "yes," we can liberate ourselves from the curse of experiencing rejection. As a matter of fact, by asking others to join us in serving, we open the door to increasing the likelihood of needs being fulfilled. For instance, if the person says they want to volunteer we may get to connect with them in a meaningful way. We mutually experience a shared desire for acceptance if we develop a quality working relationship. If the person says "no," we are just at the same place we were before, but we at least gave others an opportunity to serve.

Many times we are afraid to ask others for help. We may have experiences in our life where reliance on others was discouraged or we were taught to be self-sufficient. Yet, every person on this earth has a need to contribute to life. I believe people enjoy giving to others and are just looking for the right opportunity to do so.

You might just be the right person for the right opportunity.

When a potential volunteer cannot commit to being a volunteer you can ask them if they might know someone who can volunteer. The person may be willing to ask people they know if they are interested in volunteering, or they may be willing to give you contact information of others who may be interested in serving so that you can contact them. As you ask others to consider volunteering their time, think of it as if you are offering them a gift – the blessing to contribute.

CHAPTER SIX

AN INVITATION TO
COME AND SEE

When you ask a volunteer to serve, you are inviting them to see what volunteering at your agency is all about and to be a part of your cause. You can also have introduction nights for volunteers if they are still contemplating volunteering with your organization. It would be good to have a volunteer packet or manual for them to peruse and take home. Show professionalism by putting some thought and consideration into the program and your volunteer recruitment efforts.

It is also essential to share your organization's vision and mission with potential volunteers. The more connected they feel and the more they have the sense of being a part of a team, the better. If you have t-shirts, pens or mugs with your logo, you can give these to volunteers. When they volunteer their time, they represent the organization and you want them to believe in what they are doing. The best volunteers are the ones who are excited and proud of the service they are providing. If they like what they see and decide to jump on board, they will be grateful to have clearly defined roles and expectations.

Clearly Defined Roles and Expectations

Before any manufacturing plant or business begins anything they first need to decide what the product is that they are going to produce. Seems simple and straightforward, right? Why build a plant or start a business not knowing what your main product is going to be? It would also be important to know how to produce the product and what the finished product will look like. To start a plant or business without this information could be disastrous and very costly.

At times, organizations find themselves trying to get volunteers without knowing what the finished product is going to look like. It is essential to put some thought into why we want volunteers and what it is that we would like them to do. What do we envision volunteers doing? If it is not clear to you, it will not be clear to them. Volunteers can help you provide a service, further your mission, and play a pivotal and key role in your organization. The clearer you can be with volunteers about what you want them to do and how to do it, the better. You may want to have a role description for their position and a manual or packet that has detailed instructions on how to do tasks as well as information on things that they need to know to be effective in that role.

Background Checks and Volunteer Forms

It is important to know who you are working with so conducting background checks are essential. They can provide reassurance that someone does not have a past criminal record, that they are safe and appropriate for the role you are seeking to fill and suitable to volunteer for your organization. You also will want to have forms that gather their contact information and past work history and areas of experience. Also provide a section where they can share how they want to volunteer and how many hours they plan to contribute. This information will help you get to know prospects a bit better and it is recommended that it go in their volunteer file.

CHAPTER SEVEN

ASSOCIATION

The word 'association' in Webster's Dictionary means "to join in companionship or partnership; one who is habitually or frequently in the company or society of another. 2) To connect in thought."2 When volunteers become involved, they will be in association with you and staff. They will start to see how things work in your department and start to understand the work culture. They will also get to know your staff well. One way to train volunteers is to use time together to model what you would like them to do. They can spend hours observing you or a staff person doing a job or function for which they will eventually assume responsibility. This gives them time to catch on and integrate what they are learning. There is a saying, "Most things of importance are better caught than taught."3

When you practice modeling and leading by example the result is that it rubs off on those around you. I would prefer having someone walk with me and show me the way rather than someone just pointing me in the proper direction. Hearing a good sermon is great. Seeing one is even better.

The most effective way to train volunteers is to model the tasks and values you want them to live out. Depending on what they are doing, they may benefit more by observing the job done. Go over in detail what they are going to be doing and answer questions they have. Whenever the task or role involves something that can be observed, I recommend having the volunteer observe. Some of them may help with administration and others with direct service to others.

It is key for volunteers to see how a situation can be handled. They can learn a lot from observing how to deal with a conflict or problem. Observation can serve as a road map for when they encounter a similar circumstance. Though it is beneficial to have a manual or packet that offers step-by-step instructions or information to guide them, an effective way to learn is through modeling and one-on-one mentoring.

The more concentrated the group size being taught, the greater the opportunity for learning and for key principles to be retained. It is key to remember this point if you have over 12 volunteers.

Have you ever taken a class with only 3-12 people? It is so much easier to learn because you can ask more questions and you have more of the professor's attention. In a class where there are 250 students, it is much harder to hear and see the professor, and there's a higher chance to doze off or to not get to ask questions. Although we can have manuals and online training, it is important to not forget how effective one-on-one training and mentoring can be. When we mentor, we can model for others certain qualities, values and attitudes that a training or manual cannot cover in the same manner. Plus, we are giving our volunteers our attention and presence and building a relationship with them.

I still remember in college a friend of mine offering to teach me to change the oil in my car. He wrote down the instructions for me, but I never went through the process and changed the oil. Then one day he let me borrow some overalls and we both did it together. He modeled for me how to do it step-by-step. The next time, I did it with him observing me. I remember how impactful it was and how much easier it was for me to learn by having his supervision. The second time he made sure I had grasped how to do the task. In a similar manner, we also can check-in on volunteers and provide them feedback and supervision until they transition into the role.

A pastor I knew shared this story. He said that there were three men who went fishing together. Two of them were spiritual leaders and one of them was a new disciple. The three men went out on a boat on a lake and then one of the spiritual leaders said he forgot his lunch in the car. He proceeded to get out of the boat and walk on the water. The new disciple was flabbergasted and could not believe his eyes. The spiritual leader got his lunch and came back and walked on the water toward the boat until he got back inside. Then the other spiritual leader said it was chilly and that he was going to get his jacket. He got out of the boat and started walking on water. The leader got his jacket and walked back to the boat by walking on the water. The new disciple could not believe it. Yet, he did not say anything because he thought maybe this was a typical thing for spiritual gurus. He was embarrassed to say anything. He did not want to appear ignorant. He thought maybe there was something wrong with him since he did not walk on water. Maybe he was not "spiritual enough." Then the new disciple told the others that he, too, forgot something in the car. He then took a step into the water, thinking if they can do it he should be able to as well. As he put his foot in the water, he started to sink until he was fully submerged in the water. The two spiritual leaders each grabbed one of his arms to help him up into the boat. As one of them grabbed his arm he looked at the other leader and said, "We should have told him where the rocks are."

All that time the spiritual leaders were walking on rocks while the new disciple thought they were walking on water! Sometimes volunteers will look up to you and will see you accomplish tasks with ease. They will try to imitate you. But if they are not given instructions on where the rocks are, they will sink. Remember that they are learning from observing you, but also don't forget to explain what you are doing or why you are doing it. After giving volunteers some time to observe you, it may be time to delegate tasks to them. When they are ready, you can observe them do the role or function and give them feedback. There will come a time when the volunteer has really mastered their role or function. When this occurs, they in turn may be able to train a new volunteer. This is when we can begin to delegate more responsibility to volunteers.

In one role, I trained volunteers by having them observe me facilitate workshops and classes. One of the programs we provided was a 52-week batterer's intervention program. I found the best way to train volunteers to lead groups was for them to watch me do it for at least six months. During this time, they could ask me questions and I could have them facilitate while I observed them and provided them with feedback. It was a great environment for growth, learning and equipping. Eventually, as a result, we provided more groups as a team and we found that we had the lowest recidivism for a batterer intervention program ever known.4 One of the volunteers eventually was hired to do my job when I left the agency.

Working with Strengths

When working with volunteers we also want to discover their strengths and talents. You can of course ask them what their strengths and talents are. But as you spend time with your volunteers you will start to see their strengths and can put them in situations where they can best be used. Many times natural talents go undiscovered and people are not functioning at their best capacity. We tend to spend more time working on our shortcomings rather than developing our strong points. When working with volunteers we also want to remember not to put our focus on finding their shortcomings but to instead focus on identifying their strengths and placing them in roles where they can thrive. When working from a strengths perspective, we are at our best and there is a good chance of reaching our potential.

Fred Rogers, known as Mr. Rogers, writes, "The thing I remember best about successful people I've met all through the years is their obvious delight in what they're doing... and it seems to have very little to do with worldly success. They just love what they're doing, and they love it in front of others."[5]

I think when we are doing what we are passionate about and gifted in we are in our "sweet spot." The more I can assist others in finding that place, the more joy I experience.

I recommend checking out the book *Strength Finder 2.0* by Tom Rath. It is a book that has an assessment and can be taken online. Volunteers and staff can use it to discover their strengths. You can use the information to create teams and/or to assign tasks to individuals based on their strengths. The idea is to work with the individual's strengths, add to them and to celebrate them. When we work within our strengths we are happier and more successful and effective. Roth states in his book, "We've discovered that the most successful people start with dominant talent – and then add skills, knowledge, and practice to the mix. When they do this, the raw talent actually serves as a multiplier."6

Love Languages

Gary Chapman wrote the book *The Five Love Languages* and posits that every person has a primary way of receiving love or meeting their need for love. The five love languages are Words of Affirmation, Acts of Service, Receiving Gifts, Quality Time, and Physical Touch. When working with volunteers knowing their love language can be very helpful because we get to know how they receive care and appreciation. For instance, if a volunteer's love language is receiving gifts and you instead offer them words of affirmation, they will not have their need for care and appreciation met.

Many times we offer others what we want and what our love language is. Going back to the example of the volunteer whose love language is receiving gifts, giving them a gift card to Starbucks or a hand written thank you card will meet their need. Because everyone is different, it is beneficial to get to know how each person receives appreciation or care.

If a volunteer's love language is physical touch you can give them a fist pump, high-five or a pat on the back. Or if it is quality time, you may want to volunteer alongside them or spend time with them after they are done volunteering. You can go to lunch with them or take your break and go for a short walk. Knowing your volunteer's love language offers another way to appreciate the volunteer and to recognize them and their efforts. There is a survey that anyone can take online at www.5lovelanguages.com.

CHAPTER EIGHT

RECOGNIZING EFFORTS

"Within the community, high expectations involve believing that others can be successful, telling them so, and praising their accomplishments." – Clifton Taulbert

Whenever you have a chance to recognize the efforts of your volunteers on your team do so. This can be done in many ways. One way is to verbally acknowledge what they did and how it impacted you or the team. You can also express gratitude by telling volunteers that you are grateful for their efforts because they offered you support. You can write them a note or give them a gift card from time to time. You can also give out awards. When I had volunteers reach 100 hours of service at Mercy Housing, I made framed certificates and handed them out at a community event. I also acknowledged and honored those volunteers who gave 100 hours to our youth by framing a plaque with their name on it on our donor tree in the Youth Enrichment Room.

Additionally, t-shirts, keychains or pens with your organizations logo can also be meaningful gifts. I also would try to write press releases that highlighted volunteer's efforts. It can be very special for volunteers to find themselves on the front page of the local newspaper. These gifts are a surprise to volunteers. They are not used as an extrinsic motivator. It is important that contribution comes from a giving place in the individual. The act of giving the volunteer recognition or a gift is a way to say thank you and recognize their efforts, since for some volunteers their love language may be gifts or words of affirmation.

During *Volunteer Appreciation Week* you can take your volunteers out to enjoy a meal together. Some organizations even have a volunteer appreciation night where they hand out awards and serve dinner.

I love celebrating with volunteers the things they do that make a difference in other's lives. Whenever you have that opportunity to celebrate, take advantage of it. It is the best feeling in the world to honor another person and to see how your efforts can brighten their lives, just as they have brightened the lives of others.

Appreciation vs. Praise

When working with volunteers, or interacting with anyone for that matter, I try to give appreciation instead of praise. Before I came across Nonviolent Communication and heard Marshall Rosenberg talk about the difference between appreciation and praise, I would offer praise to people. Rosenberg shared that when we give praise to others, we stand as judge over them because we are determining if what they did was good or bad. We are the authority making the evaluation. When we practice offering appreciation, we state an observation of what the person did with no evaluation, and then note how we feel about that and how it enriched our life.

I have found that praise also falls short of what I want to really offer someone. For example, if I tell someone "Good job today!" they may not know why I am saying this. I prefer to state what someone did that enriched my life. For instance, I might say, "Today when you stayed after and helped me put things away I felt grateful because it offered me support." When I do this, the person knows exactly what I am referring to and how it impacted me emotionally. I have found that this is much more meaningful for people to receive, and it feels more genuine to me when I do it. Many people have had others use praise to try to get them to do something and when we use appreciation, we avoid being interpreted in that way.

Again, it is crucial to be specific about what that individual did that you want to recognize. For example, you can say, "I really like that you got on your knees at the child's level and gave him suggestions on how to calm down" or "I really love that you came up with the idea to work in pairs." In the former statement, you are sharing how it impacted you emotionally and what need of yours was met. In the latter, you are stating what you like by observing what they did. One more way that you can share appreciation is by expressing excitement when you give it. You can also offer appreciation through an email, a card, a voicemail message or text.

The Personal Practice of Gratitude

The practice of expressing gratitude and being thankful is a choice that unleashes positive energy into our lives. Many psychologists agree that gratitude is the healthiest human emotion. Hans Seyle claimed that gratitude produces more emotional energy than any other emotion.

Focusing on things that you are grateful for will put things in perspective and change your mood. It also keeps you from thinking negative. It produces inspiration and motivation to focus on the positive and nurture the things that really matter to us. If you put your focus on what you are thankful for, you will be more aware of the things that others are doing to enrich your life and be more capable of expressing these things to them.

Gratitude can also lift our spirit when trials come and keeps us from experiencing discouragement. Melody Beattie said, "Gratitude unlocks the fullness of life. It turns what we have into enough, and more. It turns denial into acceptance, chaos to order, and confusion to clarity. It can turn a meal into a feast, a house into a home, a stranger into a friend. Gratitude makes sense of our past, brings peace for today, and creates a vision for tomorrow."[7]

It just makes sense to be thankful. It betters our attitude and emotional experience and is a blessing for others when we express it. When we express gratitude and appreciation for what our volunteers do, it lets them know how their efforts are making a difference in our life. And because volunteers want to help, that means a lot to them.

CHAPTER NINE

SERVING LIFE

Staying connected to our values and what matters to us is important in life and important in a work culture. A focus on what serves life and contributes to the well-being of others or the betterment of the world helps us to navigate everyday situations and practice integrity in our interactions. There will be situations where we will disagree with co-workers and volunteers. It helps to focus not on what someone else did that we think is wrong or bad and instead focus on what need was not met and how we can best serve life.

Marshall Rosenberg defined good and evil in a way that helps us to see beyond the good and evil paradigm. He said that he defined good as that which serves life and evil as that which does not serve life. Many times we see things as good and evil and then categorize individuals as good or bad, and in so doing, create enemy images of others. By defining good and evil as Rosenberg does, we do not have to judge others but can determine if their actions are serving life or not. This is helpful to recall when we are giving feedback to others. We may tend to evaluate or judge others and use communication that alienates us from one another. Instead, we can evaluate if the strategies being employed are serving life (serving the organization and mission and clients).

Many times when we see someone as bad or evil we automatically think of them as the enemy, a monster or scum. This triggers anger and rarely ever leads to change or connection with the individual. It produces defensiveness.

Instead of picking sides we can simply evaluate if we or others are serving life or not. Then we can make suggestions for ourselves or others to do things that will help us or them to serve life. When I started to look at things in this way, I started to evaluate if my actions and my life were serving life. Every moment of every day we can ask ourselves, "Is what I am doing serving life?"

And if we happen to fall short we no longer need to judge ourselves and beat ourselves up by telling ourselves that we are bad. Instead, we simply mourn our actions that are not serving life and make the adjustments necessary to get our life on track. It is when we say things like "I am so horrible" that we get in trouble.

We can also evaluate if corporations, schools, churches and businesses are serving life or not. Rosenberg states that when it comes to doing things for the right motivation (to serve life) in the business world "we must be concerned that our product serves life. That our motive is not to make money but to serve life." He adds, "Don't ever, ever do anything for money but request money to meet your need for meaning."

When what we are doing is serving life we have a sense of purpose that brings peace and harmony to our lives. Max Lucado writes in the *Applause of Heaven*, "There are certain things that you can do that no one else can. Perhaps it is parenting, or constructing houses, or encouraging the discouraged. There are things that only you can do, and you are alive to do them. In the great orchestra we call life, you have an instrument and a song, and you owe it to God to play them both sublimely."8

The world needs us to find our gift or talent, and the world waits expectantly for us to not only find it but to use it to contribute to life. Many times the difficult trials that we have been through, if we learn from them, can lead to wisdom that helps us contribute to helping others. As we interact with volunteers, we can remember that we are assisting them in finding their song. If we can refrain from seeing them or others as bad, and instead focus on what serves life, we can redirect them in a non-judgmental way when they do something that we think does not serve life.

Power-with

Power-with consists of using the resources that are available to us to work with others. We mobilize resources to find ways to meet everyone's needs. There is trust and cooperation in exploring strategies that work for all parties involved. When this happens, everyone's needs matter and are held equally.

With volunteers, this may mean giving them an opportunity to participate in regular meetings where they are a part of decision-making process. It may be that you provide a setting or time for them to have a voice and feel that they can give input and feedback. If there is a concern they have about something, together you can explore ways to resolve the situation.

As a volunteer coordinator or staff working with volunteers, you are in a role where you are supervising volunteers. Likewise, you will benefit from determining a job description or role for volunteers. You can share power-with by inviting them to share their suggestions and listening to their feedback about what their role may look like. By having volunteers participate in staff meetings, it offers them an opportunity to contribute ideas or suggestions based on their experience. This can be helpful in navigating situations. Remember, volunteers can have very valuable feedback.

When we model using power-with others, and practice it with volunteers, it builds trust, inclusion, unity, and partnership.

Because power-over is modeled in many spheres in our society and power-with is less modeled, it can be hard to begin to use the power-with idea with others. It takes awareness and commitment to practice power with others. It also requires increasing our inner resources so that we have the patience, the empathy for others, and the self-control that is necessary to stay with others when things are tense. It can be helpful to have some strategies you can use to help you stay present and calm. Strategies that may assist us in increasing our inner resources include deep breathing and focusing on your breathing, taking time to disengage and calming yourself, self-empathy, focusing on feelings and needs, etc.

Miki Kashtan writes in her book *Spinning Threads of Radical Aliveness*: "By and large we have created social systems in which human needs are routinely unmet. So to prepare us to be willing to put up with such systems we must become accustomed to tolerating unmet needs from early on. This is a major aspect of the process of socialization."[9]

Intrinsic Motivation

When we focus on how what we are doing serves life, individuals, teams and departments are motivated intrinsically.

There is research demonstrating that rewards are not an effective long-term strategy in work environments because they take employees away from being motivated intrinsically. When rewards are promised or given, individuals are motivated by them, as opposed to understanding the "why" of how are their actions, thoughts, and contributions serve life.

The key is for leaders to be able to articulate the "why" behind the requests and strategies being chosen. Yet, many leaders do not have the skills to do this and instead opt for obedience and compliance with no explanation of what needs are being met by the strategies that they propose and, at times, impose.

Fear Cultures

When compliance becomes the primary focus and people are judged based upon whether or not they are compliant, a fear culture may be in the making. For example, when 100% compliance becomes the goal, we must now focus on what will happen when it is not attained. There is a higher likelihood that we will do what many of us have been socialized to do - use punishment and rewards to get others to do as we would like them to do. This breeds fear of punishment and installs competition instead of cooperation. This can drain the life out of any company or individual.

Another Way to Inspire

Inevitably, there will be times when a goal is not reached or productivity levels are not attained. When this happens, we can become curious and try to determine what is getting in the way of attaining our goals. There is usually a need or value that is not being lived out and needs attention. For instance, a team may need training or more support (staff) for volunteers to attain the goal. When we meet these needs, the likelihood that the needs of the whole will be met increase, and satisfaction or connection is also realized.

Instead of punishing, which instills fear, we can discover what strategies everyone involved can apply or need to learn in order to attain the goal. With a spirit of support and encouragement, we come alongside and learn what can help employees and teams thrive.

CHAPTER TEN

CULTIVATING EMPATHY

Rosenberg, who received the International Listening Association Listener of the Year Award, states that "empathy is a respectful understanding of what others are experiencing."

Rosenberg said that "instead of offering empathy, we often have a strong urge to give advice or reassurance and to explain our own position or feeling." He adds that, "Empathy, however, calls upon us to empty our mind and listen to others with our whole being."

Presence

I believe that empathy is about being fully present with another's experience. When we are present, we are not thinking about the laundry we need to do, the score of the baseball game or how we can get what we want. In Nonviolent Communication empathy involves imagining what the other person may be experiencing and more specifically what they may be feeling and deeply longing for or needing.

When we connect with that energy, we connect with the divine energy in the other and what really matters to them.

Organizations that help individuals, families and the community are in a position of offering empathy and healing. But it is essential for these organizations to develop a culture of empathy within the organization.

Culture of Empathy

Just like it is important for an individual to develop the habit of self-care, it is essential for an organization to develop a culture of empathy for its staff. If employees' or volunteers' buckets are on empty or close to empty, they cannot give what is needed to clients.

An organization must practice from within what it wants to demonstrate to the public or it will suffer for it. "Every employee matters and every employee's needs matter" is the motto of an organization committed to honoring needs. The same holds true with volunteers. By listening with care to the concerns and needs of individuals, the organization discovers ways to work together to better serve the community.

Finding creative ways to capture the needs of individuals, and then connecting them to the larger needs of the organization as a whole, will meet a vital need for inclusion and participation. This motivates employees to be more committed to the vision and to feel a part of the plan.

Try to offer a listening ear to volunteers by being fully present for them when they share with you. If you want, you can shift your focus to what they may be feeling and what their needs may be. If you like, you can reflect those back by saying,

"It seems like you are feeling grateful that you had the opportunity to do that because it met a need for contribution."

Sometimes volunteers may open up about something in their life with you. You can practice offering empathy in those moments. Also, if a volunteer is upset with something that may have occurred while they served for the organization and they are venting with you, you can practice offering empathy. I recommend listening and validating their feelings and needs before giving feedback or advice. For example, if someone is upset because they volunteered and someone did not say goodbye you may say, "Were you feeling frustrated when Michael walked away without saying "goodbye" because you longed for connection or to be seen?"

Or if a volunteer is upset because a client they are working with made a remark that was hard for them to hear in front of others, you could say, "I imagine you are possibly feeling hurt, embarrassed and uncomfortable because you are longing for consideration, awareness and to have more ease in your work environment?"

Offering empathy can also de-escalate situations where someone is upset. When someone is in pain, they cannot hear what you have to say. They are in too much pain. When you offer them empathy and validate their feelings and needs, their need for understanding and to be heard will be fulfilled. Usually if it is fulfilled, they will lower their voice, take a deep breath, and their body will relax. Once they are relaxed, they will be more likely to hear what you have to say.

FEEDBACK

Giving feedback to volunteers on how they are doing is an essential part of helping them grow and contribute to a shared purpose and vision. Expressing gratitude (as mentioned in the gratitude section) is an effective way of recognizing efforts volunteers are making. Giving this type of feedback is fun and generally individuals will receive this well.

Sometimes, though, people have a hard time hearing gratitude or appreciation. They may shrug off your expression of gratitude and say, "It was nothing." But the message you want to get across is that it was "something" that they did. So, in these instances, you can let them know that what they did really made a difference in your life. You repeat how what they did enriched your life or the life of others. You can also ask them if they would reflect what they heard you share. If they don't quite get it, you can tell them again until they seem to understand. Sometimes what happens when we do this is that there is a shift, and they will receive the feedback. When volunteers receive our gratitude for their efforts, we are also ensuring that they hear that they are in alignment with our shared purpose and vision.

Of course there are times when we have concerns that we want to share with a volunteer and giving them feedback is connected to helping them work on an area or to improve their service. The intention may be to help the individual be in more alignment with our goals and to support their growth in a role. If this is the case, we may need to tread more carefully. It is critical that we are calm when we express feedback. If we are upset or disappointed, we are more likely to criticize or judge the person and our body language will convey a charged energy. We may be triggered and reactive. When we share from this energy, it decreases the chances of the other person receiving our message and increases the likelihood of them getting defensive.

Assumptions

The book A Coffee Break with God shares a story about assumptions. It reads, "A traveler at an airport went to a lounge and bought a small package of cookies to eat while reading a newspaper. Gradually, she became aware of a rustling noise. Looking from behind her paper, she was flabbergasted to see a neatly dressed man helping himself to her cookies. Not wanting to make a scene, she leaned over and took a cookie herself.

"A minute or two passed, and then she heard more rustling. He was helping himself to another cookie! By this time, they had come to the end of the package. She was angry but didn't dare allow herself to say anything. Then, as if to add insult to injury, the man broke the remaining cookie in two, pushed half across to her, ate the other half, and left.

"Still fuming later when her flight was announced, the woman opened her handbag to get her ticket. To her shock and embarrassment, there was her pack of unopened cookies!"[10]

Many of us have had a situation like this occur at some time in our lives. Our perception is not always aligned with reality. We may act on the assumption that a stranger is stealing our cookies when in reality the stranger is more than willing to share his cookies with us and is offering an act of kindness.

So many times we accept our first assumptions or perceptions without even questioning them. We must be careful in our lives to not jump to assumptions about situations and instead check the facts of the situation.

When giving feedback, we want to make sure that we are not operating from assumption. An assumption is our evaluation of what has occurred that we think is true. It is a story that we create that is based on opinion and may or not be true. I have found that it does not serve me well to operate from assumption. I always want to make sure that I am connected to facts. On one occasion, while at a church service, I was whispering to my two sons to please quiet down, lower their voices and focus on their activity sheet they were given. They continued to talk louder than I was okay with and did not modify their behavior at all. I thought to myself, "How rude and inconsiderate!" My heart was racing and I was upset. I told them we were going to leave early and we did. When I got in the car I asked them why they did not listen to me with a stern voice visibly upset. They gave me a confused look and responded that the music was so loud that they could not hear what I was saying. In my head I was judging them and getting upset as a result. We talked about this and agreed that next time they would lower their voices and focus on their activity sheet. When we share an assumption with someone, they can either agree with it or disagree and usually the latter is what will happen. If there is disagreement, we are now involved in a right and wrong conversation where no one wins.

When giving feedback, I recommend first checking with the other person if they are willing to hear your feedback. I believe it will go better if they express a willingness to hear your feedback. If the willingness is not there, you may want to wait for another time where they may be more receptive. You can suggest scheduling a time to meet that works better for them. This lets them know that you are willing to consider their needs and time.

Before offering them feedback you can ask them how they think they are doing. You can ask if they see any areas or learning curve they can work on. You may find they have awareness of what to work on and it may be in alignment with what you were going to share. Providing the space for them to share in this manner allows for them to practice responsibility and can be empowering for them to experience. It also builds trust and an opportunity for them to self-discover some areas they may want to work on.

The key is to establish connection before correction. You may also share with the individual some observations of things you noticed they are doing effectively and how that has contributed to the work environment.

When you offer feedback, I recommend thinking of observations (specific, detailed things that you have observed). At times, in this setting, we may be tempted to share our thoughts and generalizations, however sharing concrete examples that we are concerned about provides clarity and shared reality. For instance, instead of saying, "You were mean with the children yesterday" an observation would be, "Yesterday during the program I noticed you raised your voice with Michael and John and told them that they were being rude."

After sharing what we are concerned about, we can share what needs or values are not being lived out as a result. This is where we share what is at stake and why this matters to us. For instance, in the above example we could say, "I am concerned because I would like for the kids to be approached with a certain level of care and tenderness and for them to be open to learning."[11]

Next, you can follow up with making clear, do-able suggestions that allow for the need to be lived out. The more specific your suggestion is, the more likely it will meet the need or value you are holding. An example would be, "Would you be willing to be aware of your tone of voice and bend down to be on the kid's level when talking to them? I find it helpful to share what I observed them do, why it matters to me, and then follow that up with a suggestion."

If you are finding that the volunteer is having difficulty receiving your feedback, they may be triggered or having a hard time receiving the feedback and you may want to offer empathy. Offering empathy in these situations helps the other person because they sense that we care about them and that we are willing to offer understanding of their experience. It shows we are not attached to an outcome and rather that we are focused on mutual understanding. When the person's need for being heard is met, they may experience relief and be ready to shift back to hearing your feedback. You can check by asking them if they would like to share anything else with you before shifting back to feedback. If they have been heard and there is nothing more they want to share, you can ask them if they are okay with hearing the feedback you want to give them. And remember to be willing to receive feedback from them, as well.

Follow Up

It is recommended to follow up with volunteers. Call or email them to see how they are doing periodically. Sometimes volunteers are shy and might be afraid to share their concerns with you. If this happens and they don't talk to anyone, they usually drop off. So, check in on them, and if you have the chance, pop in and see them in action to encourage them and to see if there is any way you can support them.

I also recommend asking them for feedback and checking if there are concerns they may have. If they do have concerns, listen and validate their feelings and needs. Consider their suggestions and try to see what you can do to resolve situations they are having.

A volunteer is giving their time away for free and if they see that you truly care about them and their concerns or feedback, they will trust you and want to continue working with you. By checking up on volunteers and meeting with them regularly, you increase the likelihood that they will continue to volunteer with your organization.

One volunteer told me that she was about to give up on volunteering because no one reached out to her after a volunteer training. The volunteer, who waited many weeks for a call, said, "When I think of the group of individuals that did the volunteer training, only a few ended up volunteering with the organization. I wonder if it was because they were not contacted for weeks. I almost was one of the ones that did not volunteer and considered moving on to another agency. But once I was connected and someone reached out to me I decided to stay because I made meaningful connections and really enjoyed my experience."

I was fortunate to connect with this volunteer by mere chance and when our paths crossed I told her about the programs I was working with and she was immediately engaged. She went on to volunteer with the agency for many years and still volunteers with the organization that I work with now. I feel very fortunate to have connected with her before she moved on to another agency!

Volunteers thrive when they know that they are valued and they matter. When you call them or follow up with them, their need for connection is often fulfilled.

CHAPTER TWELVE

RUSSELL'S STORY

When Russell is not volunteering his time at a Mercy Housing property where he lives, he can be found working on a bike to donate to a child or giving out popsicles to kids.

Russell, who is involved in helping youth at the property, facilitates the Outdoor Club on Mondays and helps with tutoring and supervision of kids during various after-school activities. It is not uncommon for kids to knock on his door to ask him for a snack or for help with something.

"I think it means a lot to the kids that he is here," a mother and resident at the property said. "The kids just love him. If he was not here they would be lost without him."

Russell started volunteering two years ago when I approached him. He was really excited about a ping pong table that was donated to the community room. I asked him to play a game and we were evenly matched. Russell kept coming back to play ping pong every day I was at the property.

After a few ping pong games and a couple of walks during our weekly Walking Club on Friday mornings, I decided to ask him if he wanted to volunteer with the kids. He kind of shrugged his shoulders and said he would think about it. A week later he said he would try it out and has been doing it since.

At first, though, Russell would only help out occasionally. I would ask him to help out with the kids and he would sometimes be there. Over time, he developed a bond with the kids and more confidence. From there he took on the Outdoor Club and became a regular volunteer with our after-school programs.

Russell is one of three volunteers at the property and one of 17 volunteers who are part of the Community Care Team that reaches out at two properties.

Mercy Housing provides affordable housing to create stable and healthy communities by developing, financing and operating affordable, program-enriched housing for families, seniors and people with special needs who lack the economic resources to access quality, safe housing opportunities.

Russell, who has made sure every child at the property got a bike, believes that it takes a community of caring people to raise a child. "It is good for families to know there are other adults that they can count on," he said.

Volunteers like Russell are individuals we can count on. I hope that as you practice these principles and tips, you cultivate volunteers who are committed, caring and connected to your mission and cause.

Swami Amritaswarupananda writes in her book *The Color of the Rainbow: Compassionate Leadership*, "Whether you are head of a family, chief of an organization, or leader of a country, if you have a caring attitude, humbleness, in approach, and the inclination to sacrifice your own personal interests and comforts (thereby truly putting the needs of others ahead of yourself), you have the traits that make you matchless. Then you will be remembered, adored, and loved as someone who truly has no replacement. Your name and your actions will always remain a guiding light to humanity."[12]

May you lead by example and guide others towards reaching their full potential. May your light shine for others to see and may your actions ignite a spark in your volunteers that heals the world.

REFERENCES

1. Swami Amritaswarupananda. *The Color of the Rainbow*. San Ramon; Mata Amritanandamyi Center, 2013.

2. Webster's Dictionary. New York; PMC Publishing Company, Inc., 1993

3. Chris Adsit, *Personal Disciplemaking*. Orlando, Campus Crusade for Christ, 1996.

4. *Batterers' Intervention Recidivism Rates Lowest Known article*. Placerville; Mountain Democrat, 2014.

5. Fred Rogers. *The World According to Mr. Rogers: Important Things to Remember*. New York; Hyperion Book, 2003.

6. Tom Rath. *Strength Finder 2.0*. New York; Gallup Press, 2007.

7. Melody Beattie. The Language of Letting Go. Hazeldon Publishing, 1990.

8. Max Lucado. *Applause of Heaven*. Word Publishing. 1990.

9. Miki Kashtan. *Spinning Threads of Radical Aliveness.* Fearless Heart Publications, 2014.

10. David C. Cook. *Coffee Break with God.* David C. Cook, 1996.

11. Marshall Rosenberg came up with a process called Nonviolent Communication that consists of making an observation, sharing a feeling and a need and making a request. This communication was referenced here and influenced my communication with volunteers. You can find more information on the process at www.cnvc.org.

12. Swami Amritaswarupananda. *The Color of the Rainbow.* San Ramon; Mata Amritanandamyi Center, 2013.

ABOUT THE AUTHOR

Eddie Zacapa was born in Santa Clara, California. He has worked with various nonprofits and is the co-founder of Life Enriching Communication and a certified trainer with The Center for Nonviolent Communication (CNVC). He also facilitates workshops where he assists individuals, couples, organizations, schools, families and communities.

He is a Resident Services Coordinator with Mercy Housing in El Dorado Hills and Shingle Springs and works with volunteers on a consistent basis. He has worked with volunteers for over 20 years with various non-profit organizations.

Eddie lives with his family in Sacramento, CA. You may contact Eddie at eazacapa@gmail.com. Eddie earned a Bachelor of Science degree in Journalism from San Jose State University and a Bachelor of Science degree in Bible and Theology from William Jessup University.

www.ingramcontent.com/pod-product-compliance
Lightning Source LLC
Chambersburg PA
CBHW051038030426
42336CB00015B/2939